AF428331

30 SECRET RECIPES FROM THE FRENCH CHEF SHRIMP-COD-SALMON-SQUID MUSSEL-LOBSTER-TROUT

William Onassis

December 2022

CONTENT

Shrimp and melon skewer with Espelette pepper

For 10 skewers you will need:

1/5 melon;

10 cooked shrimp;

1 small pinch of Espelette pepper;

10 skewers.

RECIPE:

Shell the prawns and set aside in the fridge;

Cut the melon in half, remove the seeds;

Scoop out melon balls with a spoon;

Place a shrimp and a melon ball on each skewer.

Sprinkle everything with Espelette pepper.

Cod fillet in a hazelnut crust and sherry jus

For 5 people you will need:
5 cod fillets, 130 g each;
5 tablespoons hazelnut oil for dipping;
2 full spoons and a half tablespoon of hazelnut oil for cooking;
25g butter;
5 pinches of fine salt;
5 turns of the pepper mill.

RECIPE:

Season the cod loins and place them in a dish; Brush with hazelnut oil and let stand 6-12 hours before cooking; Pan-fry the cod fillets on the skin side - just before serving - in hot hazelnut oil with melted butter for 2 minutes (fairly high heat) then place them in a dish and bake in a preheated oven at 180°C for 5 or 6 minutes; To check for proper cooking, the flesh above must be pearly.

For the hazelnut crumble, you will have:

100g butter;

100 g of blanched hazelnuts (without skin);

100g of flour;

100 g of Parmesan cheese;

1 pinch of salt.

RECIPE:

30 minutes before starting, take the butter out of the fridge and dice it (it should be soft); Coarsely chop the hazelnuts ; Mix the hazelnut powder thus obtained, the butter, the flour and the grated and sanded Parmesan by hand. Spread these crumbs on a baking sheet (covered with parchment paper) then bake in a preheated oven at 180° C for 10 minutes.

For the Sherry Vinegar Reduced Juice, you will have:

80ml sherry vinegar;

50 g powdered veal stock;

65g minced onion;

520ml of water;

120g butter.

For brown roux, you will have:

25g butter;

25g flour.

RECIPE:

Start by preparing the brown roux; melt 25g butter in a saucepan and when melted add the flour all at once; stir and cook over low heat until it looks dark golden; slice the onion very thinly; then brown the strips in 10 g of butter;

deglaze with sherry vinegar and reduce by a quarter; add water, the stock, the roux previously made and stir constantly until the preparation thickens slightly;

Then strain through a sieve to remove the onion and return to the pan; add diced butter, stirring constantly; taste and adjust the seasoning.

All you have to do is serve the cod fillets sprinkled with hazelnut crumble together with reduced juice.

Salmon, spinach and potato gratin

For 5 people, you will have:
625g fresh salmon fillets;
625 g potatoes;
250g spinach;
1 pinch of salt ;
25 cl of fresh cream (liquid or thick);
90g of cheese.

RECIPE:

Peel potatoes; cook them in boiling salted water or steam or in a pressure cooker for 13 minutes; wash spinach, coarsely drain; put them in a sauté pan with a pinch of veal stock (or salt) and cook for 4 min, covered, until they wilt; then you have to drain them; remove the skin from the salmon fillets and cut them into 1cm cubes. Place the cooked and sliced potatoes in a gratin dish ; Lightly salt them; add the drained spinach then the diced salmon; salt them very lightly again; cover with heavy cream then sprinkle with grated cheese; bake in a preheated oven at 180°C for 20 minutes. Enjoy your meal in advance!

Stuffed squid

For 5 people you will need:
1 kg squid;
170 g pork sausages;
40 g sobrassada;
1/2 garlic clove;
1 egg ;

2 tablespoons of olive oil;
4 tablespoons breadcrumbs;
1 tablespoon of flat-leaf parsley;
170 ml of milk.
170 ml of fish fumet (reconstituted with a cube

RECIPE:

Gut the squid; Then collect the pieces of flesh (the tentacles) and peel the creature (ask the fishmonger to keep the tentacles, wings and anything edible);remove the skin and cut all the pieces into small dice; turn the main part of the squid upside down like a sweater sleeve or close it with a toothpick so they don't open; mix the diced squid with the sausage meat, sobrasada, minced garlic cloves, egg, breadcrumbs and parsley; stuff the squids with this preparation very well until the end; leave about 1cm of flesh sticking out at the top; place the squid in a gratin dish; Cover with milk and fish stock; sprinkle with breadcrumbs then bake in a preheated oven at 220° C for 30 minutes. Cover with aluminum foil in case you see the breadcrumbs burning.

Mussels and fries

For 4 people you will need:
2.5 kg of mussels;
5 shallots;
1/2 bunch of parsley;
4 garlic cloves;
40g butter;

30 cl of dry white wine;
1 pinch of salt ;
1 pinch of pepper;
1 kg floury potatoes;
Frying oil ;
1 pinch of salt.

RECIPE:

For the fries:

Peel the potatoes and cut them into sticks about 1 cm wide; soak raw fries for 10 minutes in cold water to remove excess starch; take them out of the water and wipe them with absorbent paper or a clean cloth. Heat frying oil to 150° C; submerge half of the fries and cook for 10 minutes; drain well and let cool; repeat with remaining half of fries; raise the oil temperature to 180° C; before serving, dip the fries in the oil, always in 2 batches, for 5 minutes to bring them out golden brown; serve immediately with the mussels.

For the mussels:

Carefully scrape the mussels then wash them 2 or 3 times; eliminate any that rise to the surface, are broken or open; peel and finely chop the shallots; chop the parsley, peel and chop the garlic; to melt the butter; add the shallots and sauté for a few minutes; add garlic, parsley and mussels; drizzle with white wine and pepper; cover and cook over high heat for 6-7 minutes, stirring frequently; discard any that have not opened after this cooking time.

Salmon tataki

For 5 people you will need:

375g salmon fillet;	*5 pinches of sesame seeds;*
1 pinch of salt ;	*45ml soy sauce (the salty one);*
8 large Shiso leaves (Japanese groceries);	*20ml bottled Yuzu juice (at Japanese grocery stores);*
5 sprigs of chives;	*15 ml dashi.*

RECIPE:

Wash shiso leaves and chive sprigs; Pat them dry and finely chop the 2 shiso leaves and all the chives; Remove the bones from the salmon but leave the skin; Skewer the salmon with skewers; Cook it over the flame of your gas stove until the skin side caramelizes slightly and the flesh side whitens; cook about 2 minutes on the skin side and 1 minute on the flesh side; Refresh the fish in ice water for about 1 min to stop the cooking; Drain and pat dry then place in a dish; Cover with ponzu sauce and leave to rest for 30 minutes in the refrigerator.

For the ponzu sauce:

Combine soy sauce, dashi and Yuzu juice (Japanese groceries) in a bowl; Cut the salmon into slices 7-8mm thick; Place them on a shiso leaf; Sprinkle with ponzu sauce (collected in the dish), sprinkle with sesame seeds and chives. Enjoy your meal !!!

Shrimps with tomatoes, garlic and rosemary

For 5 people, you will need:
40 fresh or frozen good-sized prawns;
3 cloves of garlic;
500g cherry tomatoes;
3 beautiful sprigs of rosemary;
3 tablespoons of olive oil;
1 pinch salt.

RECIPE:

Wash the tomatoes and split them in half; Peel the garlic cloves and dice them; remove the head of the prawns and shell them; slightly slit the backs of the shrimp to remove the small black casings; wash and dry the rosemary; pour 2 tablespoons of olive oil in a sauté pan, once hot, add the half tomatoes, diced garlic, rosemary; then sauté for 7 to 8 minutes over fairly high heat; add the prawns and sauté over high heat until pink. Salt and serve immediately.

Shrimp Provençale

RECIPE:

Wash the bell pepper and cut it into small pieces; wash the cherry tomatoes and split them in half, chop the onion, wash and dry the thyme and bay leaf; pour the olive oil into a frying pan and heat, once hot (please do not smoke);

add diced peppers and onion slices; add a pinch of salt, aromatic herbs, and cook for 5 minutes before adding the tomatoes; stew another 5/7 minutes over medium heat; add peeled shrimp; add frozen shrimp to skillet; Cook for about 3 minutes, until they turn pink; Cook for 1 minute more and serve immediately. Enjoy your lunch !

Cold lobster tails with citrus fruits

For 6 people, you will need:

6 lobster tails;	*2 bay leaves;*
3 tablespoons of fennel seeds;	*1 organic orange;*
1 pinch of salt;	*1 organic lemon;*
1 pinch of pepper;	*2 cloves.*

RECIPE:

You will need 3 days to prepare your recipe.

D-2: Defrost the lobster in the refrigerator overnight;

D-1:Wash the lemon and orange, remove the zest using a vegetable peeler or vegetable peeler; Do not press too hard and just take the zest which is colored and not the white part which is bitter; Clean the bay leaves; Take a large container and add the lemon and orange zest, fennel seeds, salt, pepper, bay leaves and cloves; Add the lobster tails and cover with cold water (a little more than enough); Bring to a boil. When the water is simmering, allow 5 to 6 minutes of cooking; Remove from the heat and let the lobster tails cool in the broth overnight (at least 12 hours). Reserve in the refrigerator after 2 hours.

D-Day:

Split the lobster tails in half lengthwise; Serve cold with a delicious mayonnaise. Enjoy your lunch!

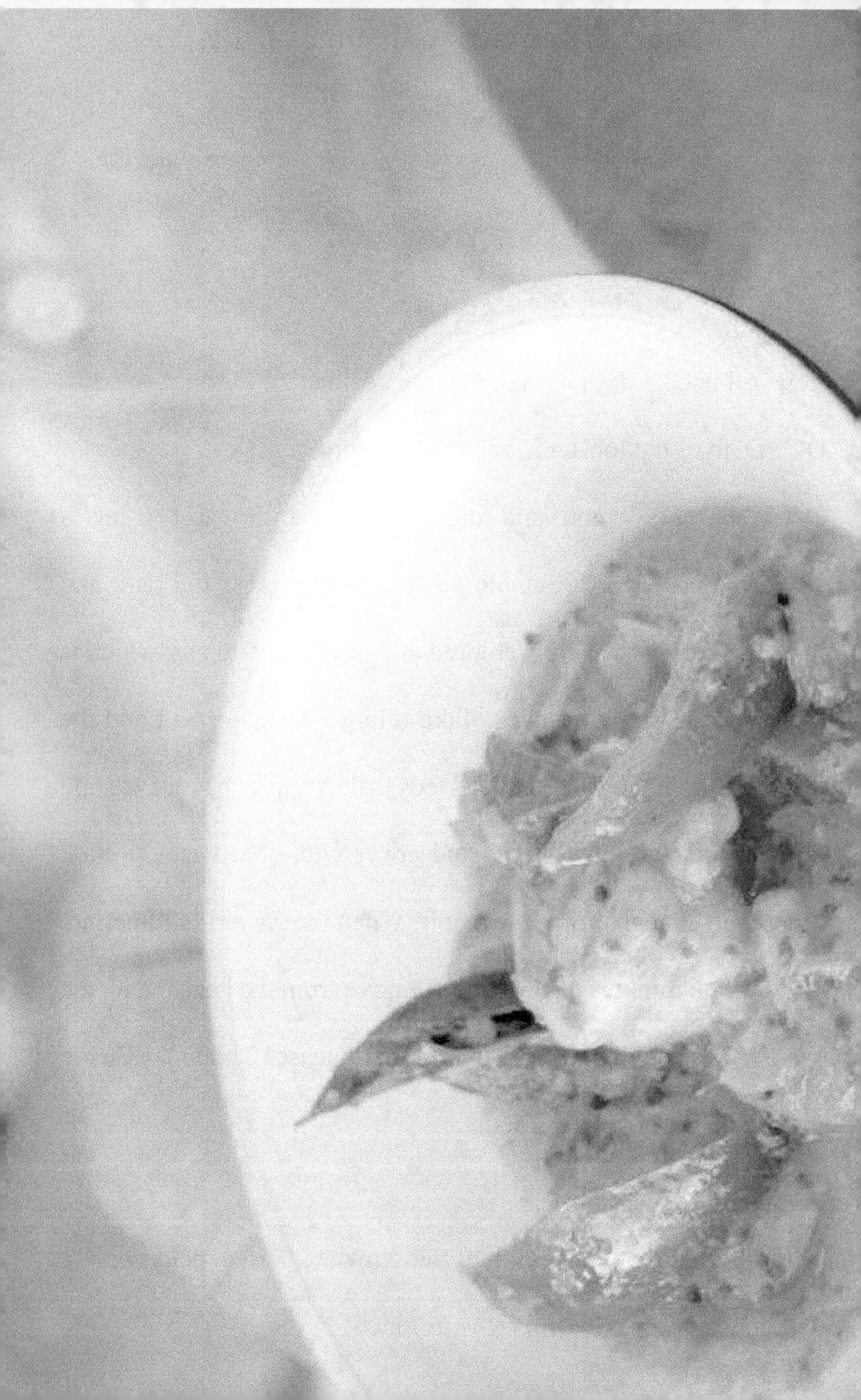

Shrimp vindaye

For 3 people, you will need:

18 raw shrimp;

5 tablespoons of olive oil;

3/4 red bell pepper;

3/4 green bell pepper;

3/4 red onion.

And for the vindaye sauce

1 and ½ tablespoons of turmeric;

5 tablespoons chopped red onion;

3 heaping tablespoons old-fashioned mustard;

2 cloves of pressed garlic;

2 pieces of ginger (about the size of the garlic clove), peeled and grated;

5 tablespoons of spirit vinegar;

8 caripoulé leaves11;

3 tablespoons oil;

1 pinch of salt.

RECIPE:

Heat 2 tablespoons of oil in a sauté pan; add the chopped red onions, chicken curry leaves, garlic and ginger, then mix; cook for about 2 minutes over low heat; reduce heat, add turmeric, cook 1 additional minute while stirring, then deglaze with vinegar; lightly salt and add mustard;

Cook for about 2-3 minutes before adding 200ml of water; mix and simmer, still on medium heat, 3-4 minutes; wash and remove the white ribs from the peppers during these 3-4 minutes;
Cut them into strips, cut the red onion into wedges; heat 1 tablespoon of oil in a sauté pan; add onion and bell pepper pieces to cook for 5 minutes, until crisp; cook shrimp over high heat for 2 minutes in oil, add to sauce, add onion/peppers mixture;

Mix, taste, add a pinch of salt if necessary and serve immediately. Treat yourself!

Fresh salmon and cucumber tartare

For 4 people, you will need:
400 g of salmon (without skin and
without stop);
200g organic cucumber;
1 red onion (30g);
2 tablespoons chopped chives.
And for the seasoning:

1 small pinch of salt;
1 pinch of pepper;
3 tablespoons lemon juice;
1 tbsp soy sauce;
1 tablespoon of runny honey;
1 tablespoon of olive oil.

RECIPE:

Cut the salmon into cubes about 1/2 cm across; wash the cucumber, do not peel it, split it in half and remove the seeds; cut it into cubes the same size as those of the salmon; wash the chives and chop them; finely dice the onion; put 1 pinch of salt, 1 pinch of pepper, honey in a salad bowl; Add lemon juice, soy sauce, olive oil and mix; Add in all the cubes (salmon, cucumber and onion) and the chives then mix gently. It would be better to serve after keeping in the refrigerator for 30 minutes or consume it immediately. Enjoy your lunch !

Trout tartare and green apple

For 4 people, you will need:
400 g of trout;
1 green apple;
1 yellow lemon;
1 teaspoon old-fashioned mustard;
1 tablespoon mayonnaise.

For the herb sauce:
1 shallot;
1 tablespoon chopped cilantro (or parsley);

1 tablespoon chopped chives;
1 tablespoon chervil;
3 tablespoons of 3 tablespoons apple cider vinegar;
8 tablespoons olive oil;
1 pinch of salt;
1 pinch of pepper.

For decoration:
1 green apple;
A little caviar.

RECIPE:

Prepare your seasoning: use a bowl, add the vinegar, salt and pepper; mix well, add finely chopped shallot, mustard, olive oil; gently stir and incorporate the herbs, then set aside; wash the green apple and cut it into small pieces, add lemon and set aside; dice trout and place in a bowl; add the mayonnaise, the apple sticks then very gently fold in the herb vinaigrette; taste and adjust the seasoning if needed; to serve, arrange with a ring and place on top of the tartare, a few sprigs of chervil and a slice of green apple; add 1/2 teaspoon of caviar on top of the tartare. Enjoy your meal in advance !!!

Leek and two salmon tart

For 1 pie you will need:

750g white leeks;
300g fresh salmon;
100 g smoked salmon;
2 organic eggs;

300 g Philadelphia type cream cheese;
100 g grated Gruyère cheese;
1 ready-made pure butter or homemade shortcrust pastry.

RECIPE:

Split the leek whites in half, wash and cut into strips; pressure cook them for 10 minutes then set aside; preheat oven to 210°C; remove salmon skin and bones; then cut it into cubes of about 1.5 cm side; also cut the smoked salmon into evenly sized squares; pour cream cheese into a bowl; add the eggs then mix; add diced salmon and pre-cooked leeks; put the dough in a mold, prick it with a fork; pour the mixture inside and sprinkle with grated cheese; bake for 30 minutes then serve warm, hot or cold with a green salad.

N.B.: Do not add salt because smoked salmon is already salty.

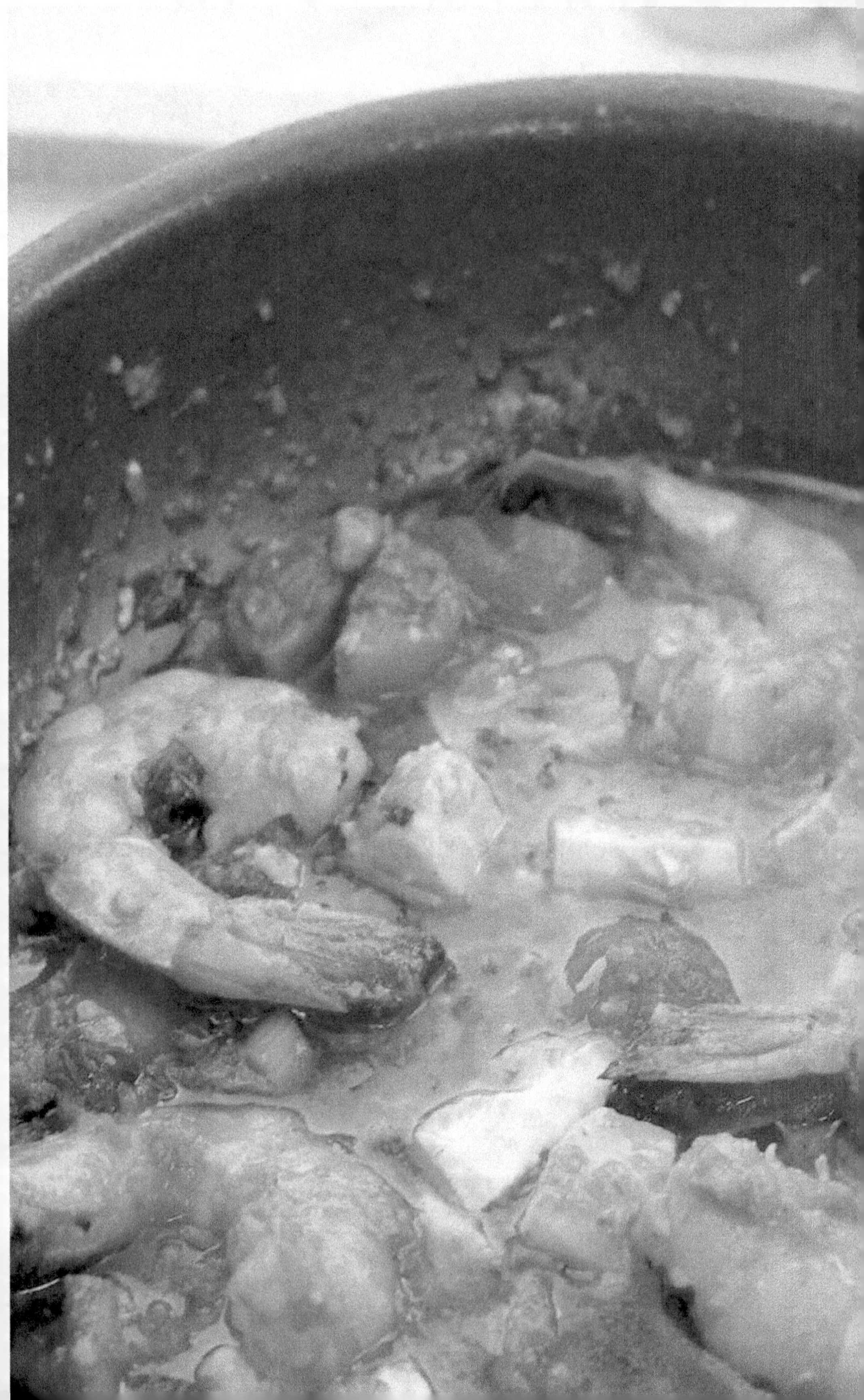

Saganaki Shrimps

For 3 people, you will need:

6 large peeled prawns;
3 tablespoons of olive oil;
3 new onions (or 1 classic);
1 and ½ cloves of garlic;
1 and ½ tablespoons of aniseed
alcohol (ouzo, pastis…);
1 and ½ tablespoons of white wine;
1 and ½ tomatoes;
9 cherry tomatoes;

8 tablespoons Neapolitan tomato sauce
(ready-made is fine);
3 teaspoons of capers;
1 pinch of salt;
1 pinch of oregano;
3 teaspoons chopped parsley;
150 g feta, diced;
75ml of water.

RECIPE:

Peel the onions and chop them; peel the garlic clove, degerminate it and press it; wash and peel the tomato, remove the seeds and cut into cubes; wash the cherry tomatoes and split them in half; heat 3 tablespoons of olive oil in a frying pan over high heat, as soon as it is hot, add the prawns, sear them for 1 to 2 minutes then add the diced onions and the pressed garlic ; pour in ouzo and white wine; mix then add the crushed tomato, cherry tomatoes, tomato sauce, capers, a pinch of salt and 1 pinch of oregano; stir, add water, parsley and 150g diced feta; leave to cook for another 2 minutes, the feta falling apart in places will thicken the sauce.

Prawns with pineapple and curry

For 4 people you will need:

400g prawns (fresh or frozen);

450g pineapple;

1 large onion;

2 cloves garlic ;

1 tbsp curry powder;

1/2 teaspoon powdered ginger;

1 knife tip of Espelette pepper;

20 cl of coconut milk;

1 pinch of salt ;

4 tablespoons of olive oil;

1 tbsp sprigs of coriander or parsley;

1 lime.

RECIPE:

Peel the onion, cut it into strips; peel the garlic cloves, degerminate them and dice them; wash and dry cilantro or parsley; fry the pineapple cubes over a very high heat in a non-stick sauté pan for 5 minutes, stirring them two or three times; the diced pineapple will be all golden and almost caramelized then put them in a ramekin; remove the heads from the prawns and shell them; using a knife, slit the back slightly and remove the small black casing; pour 2 tablespoon olive oil into same sauté pan used with pineapple; heat and sauté shrimp 4-5 minutes over high heat, until pink and golden, then set aside in a ramekin; pour another 2 tablespoons of olive oil into the same pot; heat and brown the garlic and onion slices over medium-high heat for about 4 minutes. Then add the curry, ginger, Espelette pepper, salt and mix; after 1 to 2 minutes, pour in the coconut milk, continue to heat for 1 minute then add the diced pineapple and the prawns to the mixture;

Mix and heat for 2 minutes, then sprinkle with coriander sprigs or parsley and accompany the dish with a piece of lime.

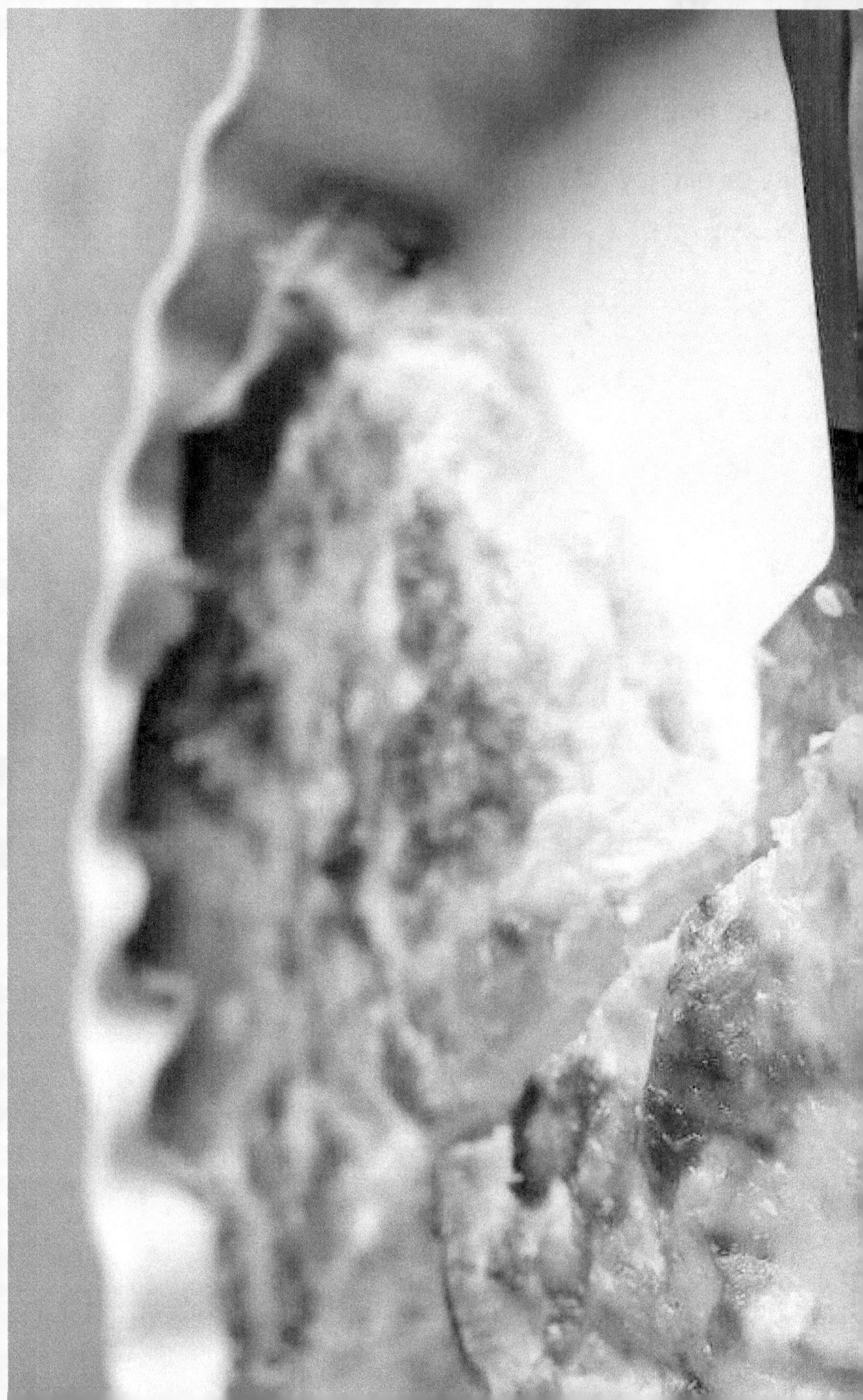

Leek and two salmon quiche

For 6 people, you will need:

500g white leeks;

150ml dry white wine;

1 chicken stock cube;

2 tablespoons whipping cream;

15 g butter;

1 pinch of salt ;

250 g fresh organic salmon;

90g diced smoked salmon;

300 g Philadelphia type cream cheese;

2 eggs ;

1 shortcrust pastry, homemade or purchased;

75 g grated Emmental cheese.

Start by cutting the stems of the leeks, remove the first damaged leaves, split them in half and clean them carefully, then cut them into strips; melt the butter in a sauté pan, once melted, add the leeks, a pinch of salt and cook for 5 minutes over high heat; then add the chicken stock cube, the white wine and cook for about twenty minutes over medium heat; there should be no liquid left at the end, if there is not enough, add a little water or white wine; At the end of cooking, add 2 tablespoons of whipping cream and set aside; remove skin from salmon, cut into approximately 2cm dice; toss with diced smoked salmon; preheat the oven to 210° C; crack 2 eggs into a bowl, beat them into an omelette; add cream cheese, then mix; add well-drained leeks and both salmon; spoon batter into pan, prick lightly with fork; pour egg/cheese/salmon/leek mixture over batter; cover with grated cheese and bake for 30 minutes; in case the quiche is not golden enough, add 3 to 4 minutes of cooking under the grill position and watch closely that it does not burn.

Enjoy your lunch!!!

Chicken curry with prawns

For 6 people you will need:

4 chicken cutlets;
10 large prawns;
3 tablespoons of olive oil;
1 clove of garlic;
1 onion ;
2 tablespoons curry powder;

1 chopped chilli (optional);

40ml of water;
1 pinch of salt ;
3 tablespoons of yogurt.

RECIPE:

Peel the garlic, onion and remove the skin from the tomato; chop the garlic, finely chop the onion and dice the tomato; cut the chicken cutlets into pieces about 2-3cm across; shell the prawns and remove the black vein;

pour 3 tablespoons of olive oil into a hot skillet; add garlic, onion and cook over high heat. Add the chicken cutlets and prawns and brown well, still over high heat; when the chicken pieces are colored on all sides, add the curry powder and simmer for 2 minutes; then add the chopped chilli, diced tomatoes and water, then lightly salt; then add the yogurt and simmer for 3 to 4 minutes before serving hot, the dish can be served with white rice!

Baked sea bream with orange and lemon

For 4 people, you will need:
1 sea bream, about 1.5 kg, scaled and gutted;
6 organic oranges;
2 lemons;
1 red onion;
3 tablespoons of olive oil;
1 pinch of salt ;
1 pinch of pepper.

RECIPE:

Preheat oven to 180° C; wash and dry the sea bream; Brush with olive oil, season with salt and pepper and place in a baking dish; wash an orange, dry it and slice it into rounds about 0.5 cm thick; peel the red onion and also cut it into strips the same size as the orange, arrange it all over the sea bream; season with salt and pepper, squeeze the juice from 5 oranges and 2 lemons then pour the juice over the sea bream; place in the oven and cook for 30 minutes, basting at least twice; while another person fillets the fish, collect the juice and reduce it over high heat by half; serve the fish with this sauce and with rice in which you will put the slices of orange and red onion.

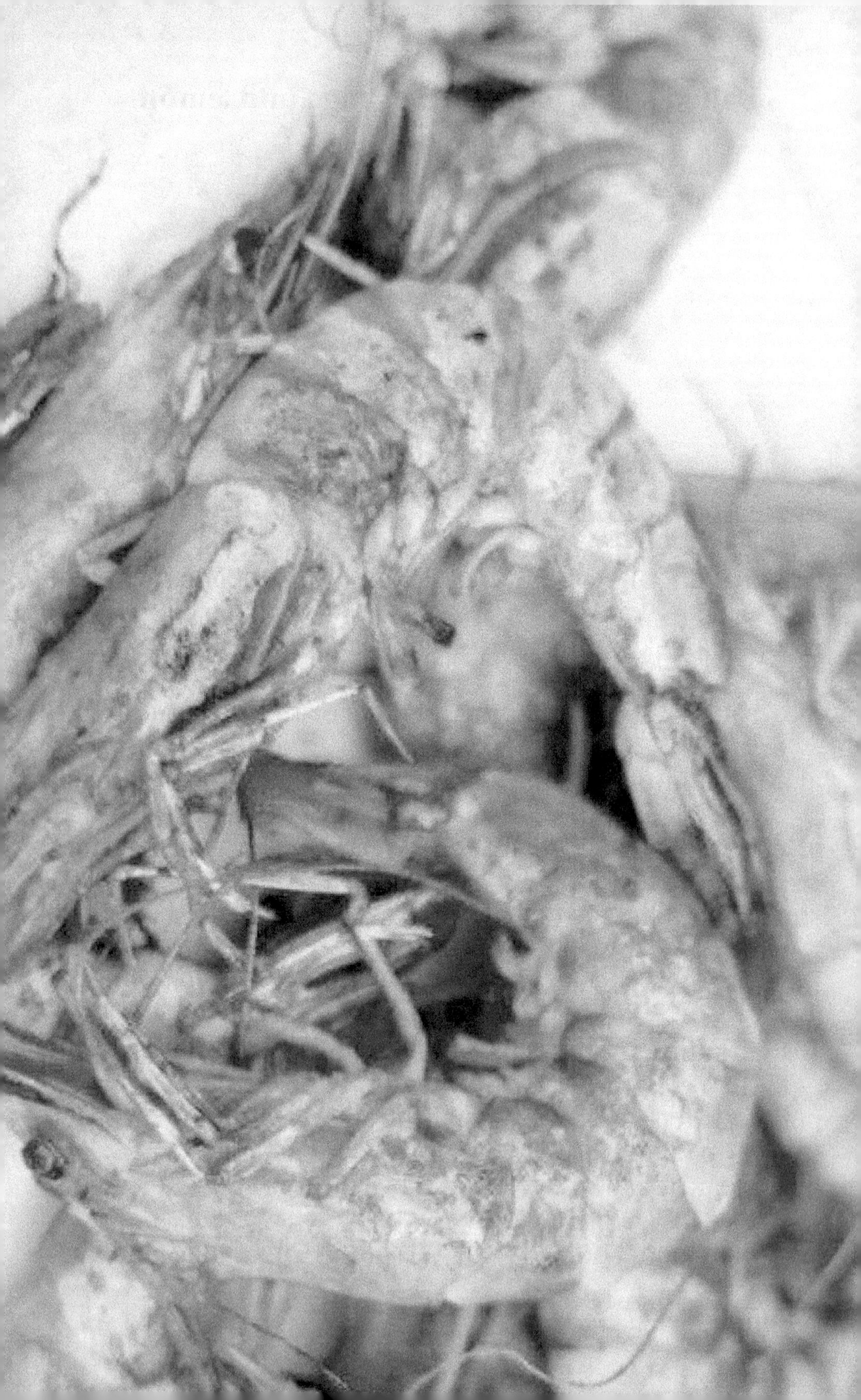

Prawns with vanilla olive oil and lime

For 5 people you will need:

25 king prawns;

60 ml vanilla olive oil;

1 lime juice;

1 pinch of salt.

RECIPE:

Place the prawns in a large dish; drizzle with olive oil and lime juice; mix and let marinate for at least 30 minutes in the refrigerator; light the plancha to a high heat; add the prawns and cook for 2 minutes on each side, basting them with the marinade; return the cooked prawns to the dish, season with salt and serve hot;
Enjoy !!!

Lacquered salmon soy sauce with mangoes, star anise and lime

For 2 people, you will need:
2 salmon fillets of 150g each (skinless);
1 mango;
1 organic lime;
1 tbsp chopped cilantro or parsley;
150ml soy sauce;
1 star anise (star anise).

RECIPE:

Preheat the oven to 180° C; Peel the mango and dice it; Put them in a bowl, add the star anise and sprinkle with soy sauce. Marinate 5 minutes; Place halved salmon fillets in two ramekins; Divide diced mangoes and soy sauce evenly; Bake for 10 minutes; Meanwhile, wash and zest the lime, chop the parsley or cilantro; Once the salmon is cooked; Sprinkle it with the coriander or parsley and the lime zest. Serve hot, accompanied by a bowl of Basmati or Thai rice.

Salmon Tartare with Basil and Wasabi

For 4 people, you will need:

4 salmon steaks,
150g each, organic or label rouge;
1 red onion;
1/2 bunch of basil;
1 organic lemon;
3 pinches of salt;
2 pinches of Espelette pepper;
1 heaping tablespoon of olive oil;

1 pinch of wasabi powder.
To accompany, you will have:

3 tablespoons of olive oil;
50ml rosé Crémant de Bordeaux;
20 g of honey;
3 pinches of salt;
3 turns of the pepper mill.

RECIPE:

First start removing the salmon fillets and then remove the skin; cut the flesh of the fish into small cubes; zest and juice the lemon; chop red onions and basil; combine the salmon, in a bowl, red onions, basil, lemon juice and zest, espelette pepper, fine salt, olive oil and wasabi powder; arrange mixture in cookie cutter on plate; wash the sucrines and split them in half; heat the plancha then pour olive oil on it. Once hot, lay the lettuces, flat side down; as soon as they are colored, turn them over on the domed side; drizzle with honey and deglaze with crémant; reduce until glazed then season with salt and pepper; arrange the sucrines next to the tartare, add a few mesclun leaves if you wish and enjoy. Enjoy!

Plancha of caramelized salmon and crunchy Chinese cabbage

For 4 people, you will need:

500g Skinless Red Label Scottish salmon fillet, cut into slices approximately 5mm thick;
15 cl of soy sauce;
1 tablespoon of runny honey;

400 g Chinese cabbage;
5 cl of olive oil;
2 tablespoons rice vinegar;
1 pinch of salt ;
1 pinch of ground pepper.

RECIPE:

Mix the honey with half the olive oil, half the soy sauce and pepper all in a bowl; finely chop the Chinese cabbage; mix it in a bowl with the rest of the olive oil, the rice vinegar, the rest of the soy sauce, salt and pepper then set aside in the fridge; push a wooden skewer into the salmon slices; season it with salmon, grill it for 1 minute on each side on the griddle or in a non-stick pan (without fat); pour the honey and soy mixture over the pieces of salmon, let caramelize for a few seconds then serve immediately with the crunchy Chinese cabbage salad.

Grilled salmon with cream cheese and chives, zucchini with sesame

For 4 people, you will need:

4 skinless Red Label Scottish salmon steaks, about 160 g;
150 g fresh cheese;
1 bunch of chives;
10 cl of olive oil;

40 g sesame seeds;
4 round zucchini;
1 pinch of salt ;
1 pinch of ground pepper

RECIPE:

Preheat the oven to 180° C, thermostat 6; wash and cut the zucchini in half; store them in a baking dish; Season, drizzle with half the olive oil, then sprinkle with sesame seeds; bake the zucchini for 20 minutes in the oven; split salmon steaks in half, thickness wise; season them then mix the cream cheese in a bowl with the chopped chives, salt and pepper; stuff the inside of the salmon steaks with the fromage frais; cook the salmon steaks 4 to 5 minutes on each side in a skillet in the remaining olive oil over medium heat; serve immediately with the sesame zucchini.

Enjoy your meal in advance!

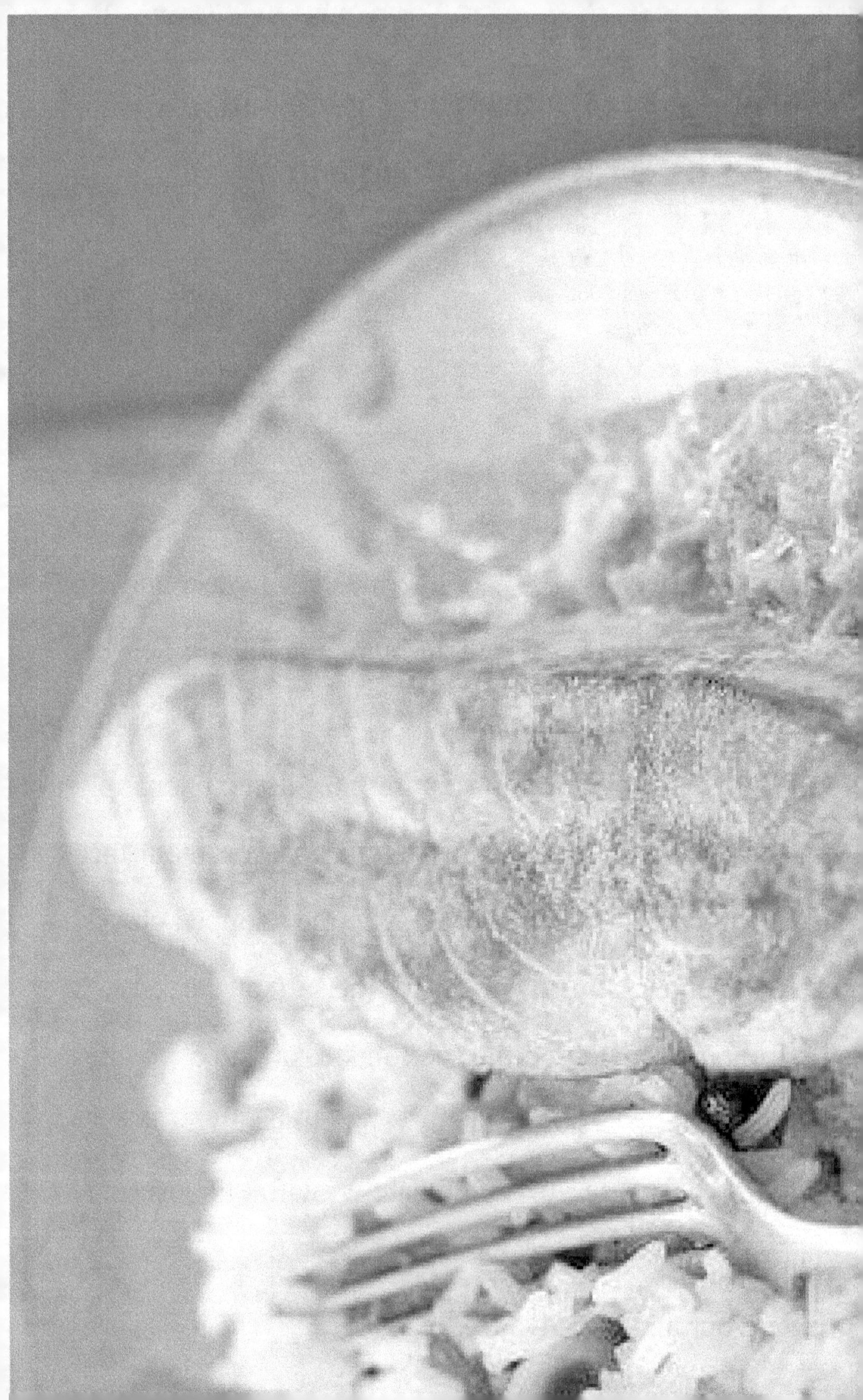

Salmon steak with green curry and cashew nuts

For 4 people, you will need:

*4 pieces of red label Scottish salmon,
about 160 g without skin;
70g green curry paste;
50 g cashew nuts;
1 onion ;*

*5 cl of olive oil;
20 cl of coconut milk;
2 sprigs of fresh cilantro;
1 pinch of salt ;
1 pinch of ground pepper.*

RECIPE:

Carefully open the salmon steaks in the direction of the thickness in portfolio; spread half of the green curry inside, salt and pepper the steaks; coarsely chop the cashews; peel and chop the onion; melt it for 5 minutes in half the olive oil in a saucepan over low heat; add cashews and remaining green curry; let brown for 2 minutes then add the coconut milk and 5 cl of water; season with salt and pepper and cook for 10 minutes over medium heat, stirring regularly; add the chopped coriander at the end of cooking then keep the sauce warm without boiling it; cook the salmon steaks for 4 to 5 minutes on each side in a pan in the remaining olive oil over medium heat. Serve the salmon steaks with the sauce, accompanied with fried rice with almonds.

ubes of salmon with roasted seeds, celery and crunchy carrot curry

For 4 people, you will need:

450g Skinless Red Label Scottish Salmon Fillet;
20 g blond sesame seeds;
20g black sesame seeds;
30 g flax seeds;
200 g carrots;
200g celeriac;

10 cl of olive oil;
2 lemon juice;
3 tablespoons of wine vinegar;
1 tablespoon walnut or hazelnut oil;
1 teaspoon of curry;
1 pinch of salt ;
1 pinch of ground pepper.

RECIPE:

Mix half the olive oil in a bowl with the walnut or hazelnut oil, lemon juice, salt and pepper; cut the salmon fillet into approximately 1.5cm x 1.5cm cubes; place them in a dish, pour the marinade over them; place salmon in refrigerator, marinate chilled 30 minutes; toast the seeds 3 to 4 minutes in a frying pan without fat to roast them; peel and grate the carrots and celery; season with remaining olive oil, vinegar, curry, salt and pepper; remove salmon cubes from marinade; toss them in the roasted seeds to coat them; serve the salmon with the grated vegetables.

Salmon tournedos with fresh herbs

For 8 people, you will need:

1 nice fillet of salmon, organic or label rouge;

1/2 bunch of parsley;

1/2 bunch cilantro;

heat resistant plastic wrap;

1 large pinch Espelette pepper;

1 pinch of salt ;

3 tablespoons of olive oil.

RECIPE:

Start by removing the skin from the fish fillet or ask your fishmonger to perform this operation when buying, remove the bones using pliers; also remove the slightly gray parts of the salmon, if there are any; split the thickest part of the fillet (about 3/4 of the length) about 2 cm deep along the backbone; then fold the fish in half to form a sausage;

Cut a plastic film and make a bed of herbs; place salmon fillet on top and start rolling; add a lot more plastic wrap so the net is tight; then close the sausage at each end with a tie; refrigerate 15 minutes;slice your sausage into 6 equal-sized sections; preheat oven to 180° C, just before baking; pour 3 tablespoons of oil into a skillet; to heat ; sear the salmon tournedos for about 2 minutes on each side; sprinkle with espelette pepper when colored;

Then place the tournedos on a baking sheet lined with a silicone mat or baking paper; cook for 10 minutes, remove the plastic film, salt and serve !

Salmon marinated in olive oil

For 4 people you will need:

1 piece of salmon 400g without skin
or bones (the back part of a salmon);
2 tablespoons coarse sea salt;
2 tablespoons of sugar;
2 tablespoons cracked pepper.

To serve:
2 tablespoons chopped chives;
4 tablespoons fruity olive oil;
Lemon wedges;
toast.

RECIPE:

Rinse the piece of salmon and pat it dry; put it on a plate and sprinkle it with sugar, salt and pepper on both sides; cover it with cling film and put it in the fridge; let it macerate for 3 hours; remove fish from cold, rinse thoroughly to remove all salt and sugar; pat it dry and cut it into thin slices; divide fish slices among four plates; drizzle with oil and sprinkle with chopped chives; garnish with lemon wedges; serve immediately with slices of toasted bread.

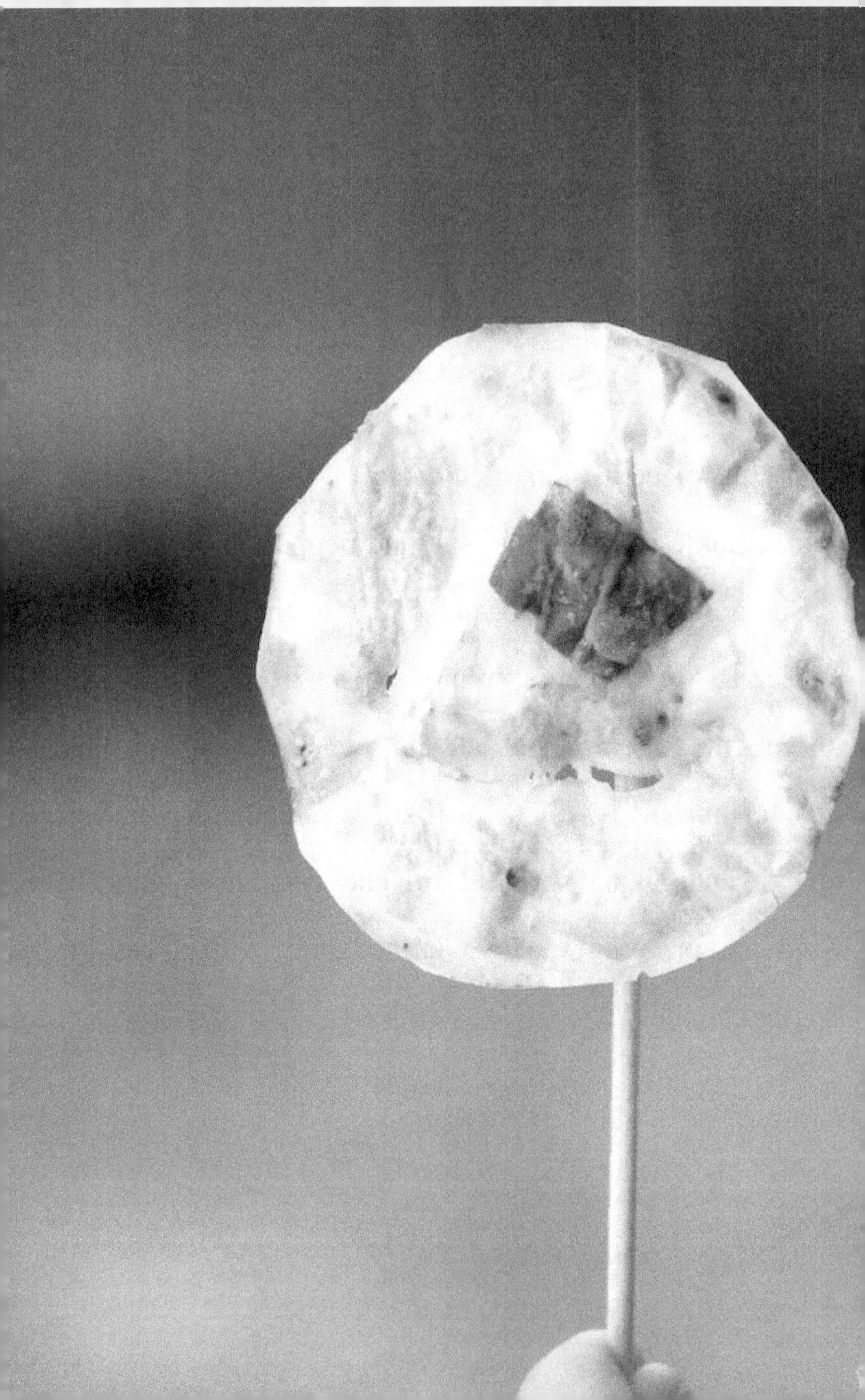

Crispy langoustine lollipops with basil

For 24 lollipops, you will need:

12 raw medium langoustines;
8 brick sheets of 30 cm;
12 basil leaves;
10cl olive oil;

Salt;
Espelette pepper;
24 sticks.

RECIPE:

Shell the raw langoustines, removing the head, tail and shell; cut them in half lengthwise and remove the black casing; cut the pastry sheets using a cookie cutter (8cm in diameter) to obtain 48 circles; brush half with egg yolk; place on top 1/2 basil leaf, 1/2 langoustine, 1 pinch of salt, 1 pinch of Espelette pepper then seal tightly with another disc of dough; do this until you run out of ingredients; in a non-stick skillet, drizzle olive oil, heat over high heat; cook all double-sided bricks for about 1 minute on each side; the lollipops should get a nice golden color; at the end, remove them to absorbent paper and slide a 10 cm long wooden spade into each pastry sheet to make it a lollipop; pour into a glass and then serve immediately.

Smoked salmon cheesecake

For 3 cheesecakes (diameter 7 cm) you will need:

225 g cream cheese;

3 slices of smoked salmon;

90g savory crackers;

3 teaspoons candied lemon;

1 tablespoon powdered ginger;

1 pinch of Espelette pepper;

45 g salted butter;

3 tablespoons of olive oil;

75ml single cream;

1 gelatin sheet (2 g);

3 tablespoons chopped chives.

For the decoration you will need:

9 pink berries;

1 tablespoon chopped chives;

1 pencil of beet and ginger coulis;

1 lemon cut in 6.

Soak the gelatin sheet in a bowl of cold water; minely dice the candied lemon; wash and chop the chives; blend crackers in food processor; add powdered ginger and espelette pepper; meanwhile melt the butter; once melted, add it to the cracker crumbs, pour in 2 tablespoons of olive oil and blend again; line 2 stainless steel circles 7 cm in diameter with parchment paper; lay a parchment paper on a flat surface then place the three circles on it; divide the cracker mixture between the 2 circles then pack well; keep cool; pour the cream cheese into a bowl then loosen it with a whisk; heat the liquid cream and add the drained gelatine sheet;

Mix well then fold this mixture into the cream cheese; whisk lightly then stir in the chives, diced lemon confit and chopped chives; remove circles from refrigerator; pour this preparation evenly between the 2 circles; freeze 1 hour while cheesecake hardens; when ready to serve, garnish the plate with drops of ginger beet coulis; cut 3 pieces of smoked salmon the diameter of the circle; remove the cheesecakes from the pans, place the circles of salmon on top of the cheesecakes;

Put them in the pre-decorated presentation plates; sprinkle with a few grains of crushed pink berries and a few sprigs of chopped chives; serve immediately with a lemon cut in 6. Enjoy!!!

Shrimps with spicy sauce

For 3 people you will need:

600 g fresh, peeled prawns;
1 and ½ tablespoons of oil + 1
teaspoon of sesame oil;
1 and ½ tablespoon curry powder;
4 tablespoon of chili sauce (jelly-like
with chili sauce crumbs);
4 tablespoons of lemon juice;
2 bell peppers;
1 tomato;
1 clove of garlic.

RECIPE:

Place shrimp to marinate in a bowl with oil, sesame oil, curry, chili sauce soup and lemon juice; Chill them for about 1 hour in the fridge; Meanwhile, sauté the green pepper strips and tomatoes in a wok with a little oil; Add a clove of pressed garlic.

When the vegetables are golden, add the prawns and their marinade and allow time for them to turn pink; Season with salt and pepper, then serve.

Enjoy your lunch !

GLOSSARY

Espelette pepper : variety of pepper of West Indian origin, straight and elongated shape used as a condiment in the kitchen.

Vinegar of Xerxes : variety of Spanish vinegar of exceptional quality.

Soubressade : cured meat of Spanish origin, in the form of sausage and known as Sobrassada de Mallorca.

Shiso Leaf: The lacy leaf of a Japanese plant called Shiso or Perilla Frutescens, used in cooking for flavoring.

Yuzu juice: juice obtained from the leaves of Yuzu (plant of Japanese origin).

Dashi: Seaweed and bonito broth made together and is the basis of Japanese cuisine.

Ponzu sauce: Japanese sauce made from sour Japanese citrus fruits.

Fennel Seeds: Large streaky pale green-yellow seeds collected after the fennel blooms.

Vindaye: fish-based dish of Mauritian origin.

Caripoulé: leaves of Karipoulé (tropical climate citrus fruit native to Reunion Island).

Organic Cucumber: Organically grown cucumber.

Apple Cider Vinegar Soup: Soup made from Apple Cider Vinegar.

Shrimp Saganaki: dish of Greek origin.

Star anise (or star anise): fruit of the Chinese star anise, used as a spice in cooking for its aniseed taste.

Wasabi: paste obtained from a plant of Japanese origin of the same name.

Plancha: hot metal plate used to sear food.